D0241682

NOTE TO PARENTS

Rainbow Guides are the youngest and newest members of the worldwide family of Guides. The section was created as a result of the increasing pressure from girls who 'could not wait' to become Brownies!

As a parent of such a girl, you will know that she is full of energy, has plenty to say and can be, at times, almost irrepressible. At other times, though, she can be quiet and extremely thoughtful; this is because she is working out ideas and issues for herself.

The Rainbow Guide programme is designed to help girls of this age through this stage of development so that they are able to become Brownie Guides who can cope with new situations and who are confident enough to make new friends and try different activities.

This book is intended to be shared by parents and girls so that both understand a little more about Guiding and particularly the Rainbow Guide section. Read and enjoy it together so that your daughter's membership of a worldwide Movement is an enjoyable and meaningful experience which will continue throughout her childhood and, we hope, adult days.

Betty Stevens
Rainbow Guide Adviser 1986–90

I'm a Rainbow Guide

written by Gill Pawley
illustrated by Helen Herbert
prayer on page 22 written by Rev M Shapland

Copyright © 1991 The Girl Guides Association.
All rights reserved.
Published in Great Britain by World International Publishing Limited,
an Egmont Company,
Egmont House, PO Box 111, Great Ducie Street, Manchester M60 3BL.
Printed in Germany. ISBN 0 7498 0190 5

A CIP catalogue record for this book is available from the British Library.

Hello! My name is Katie. I'm nearly seven years old and I'm a Rainbow Guide.

Rainbow Guides are the youngest members of the family of Girl Guides, which also includes Brownies, Guides and Rangers.

I am Naomi – I'm five and I'm nearly a Rainbow.

Rainbow Guides are little girls who are too young to be Brownies. When we are seven we can move on to Brownies.

Here are our Guiders. Their names are Swallow, Jackdaw and Robin. There is also Sally, who is a Young Leader.

Our Guiders organize meetings for us and plan what we are going to do each week. They look after us and we do lots of exciting things together.

All Rainbow Guides make this Promise:

"I will do my best to love God and to be kind and helpful."

You make your Promise soon after you join Rainbows. Then you can wear the Rainbow Guide badge.

All Rainbow Guides wear a special tabard over ordinary clothes. Ours is red, but tabards can be any rainbow colour. We think our uniform is great!

Each week we play games. Sometimes we are in teams or groups. At other times we play with a partner, or all together. The games are great fun, and we all take turns and share things like balls and ropes.

We enjoy making things and sometimes we make presents we can give to other people, like our mums, dads or grans.

Here we are making pencil holders.

I like it when we sing songs. Jackdaw plays her guitar and we get a chance to play some instruments like drums and shakers.

My favourite part of Rainbow meetings is when we have a story. Swallow often reads to us and sometimes we join in. I really enjoy stories where all the Guiders join in to play a part.

Everyone likes it when we have a visitor at a meeting. We have met a policewoman, a nurse and a lady who makes dolls.

Rainbow Guides enjoy helping. We like to go to visit a home for old people. Sometimes we take small presents we have made.

At our Rainbow Guide meetings we learn how to help other people. We try to remember this at home. We help to tidy up and put our toys away.

We sometimes go out together. It's great fun! Last summer we went on a picnic. We have also been out in small groups with Robin to learn the Green Cross Code.

At the end of our meetings we say a prayer. Sometimes we say this one:

Thank you God for Rainbows.
Thank you for our leaders.
Thank you for each other.
Please help us to keep our
Rainbow Promise.
Please watch over us and keep us
safe until we meet next time.
Thank you God.
Amen.

Sometimes there is a special evening for mums and dads so they can see what we do at Rainbow meetings. Swallow usually makes a display of some things we have made. We play games and sing songs for our parents and friends.

Everyone must help to tidy up at the end of our meetings. We have a cupboard where we keep everything and it must be kept tidy. Sally knows where everything should go.

Because other people (like the Brownies and Guides) also meet in the community centre, we must be careful to leave the hall neat and clean.

Katie is seven now and it is time for her to move to Brownies. She says goodbye to all her friends in Rainbows.

Brownies wear yellow and brown uniforms. They are split into groups called Sixes with names like Gnomes, Elves, Sprites and Pixies. Katie will be in the Gnomes. Each Six has a leader called a Sixer. Katie's Sixer is Donna. Brownies work for different badges and do many exciting things.

We hope you have enjoyed reading about Rainbow Guides. Goodbye!